JAPANESE
Jive

JAPANESE Ji

Wacky and Wonderful Products

First edition, 1993
Second printing, 1994

Published by Tengu Books
420 Madison Avenue, 15th Floor
New York, N.Y. 10017

© 1993 by Caroline McKeldin; all rights
reserved.

Cover, book design and typography by Liz
Trovato

Printed in Hong Kong

ISBN 0-8348-0278-3

Contents

foreword
by
George Fields

"Never mind what it means. Does it sound good?"

During my years of explaining the Japanese market to the West, the question most often asked me has been "Why are so many brand names in English?" The standard and perhaps simplest explanation rests on the link between use of Western languages and the goal of modernization. While Japan was working to pull a closed, feudal society into the twentieth century, having foreigners around and using foreign words somehow showed that progress was being made. Of course, much of this linguistic transformation was simply cosmetic, but unless one mixed with live foreigners and really understood English, which few Japanese did, the appearance of internationalization was there: using English was modern.

But, of course, there's much more to it . . .

After spending my early years in Japan and attending Japanese schools up to senior high, I was cut off from the country and the Japanese language almost completely for two decades. When I finally went back to Japan, I shared with Rip Van Winkle and his Japanese counterpart, Urashima Taro, the experience of returning to my community after the lapse of a generation. I found the Japanese I had acquired earlier was superficially adequate, but to really understand my old friends I had to learn the plethora of new words that had entered the lexicon in my absence. Most these new words were of English derivation, many brought into

use because there was no equivalent Japanese for a concept; for example, since the Japanese had never lived in "privacy" the new word for it was the borrowed *puraibashii*.

Important in this borrowing process is a fundamental characteristic of the Japanese language itself, which is communicated through five basic vowel sounds: *a*, *i*, *u*, *e*, and *o*. Consonants placed in front of these create other syllables. Placing *k* in front gives *ka*, *ki*, *ku*, *ke*, *ko*; adding *b* produces *ba*, *bi*, *bu*, *be*, *bo*, etc. When foreign words are borrowed, they are rendered into these basic sounds; it is not necessary to pronounce them as in the original language. "Aspirin," for example, is *asupirin*; "socks" are *sokkusu*. This is a very handy system for acquiring foreign words quickly and in great numbers. Pronounce an English word the Japanese way—*sutē-shon* for "station" or *tonneru* for "tunnel," for example—and chances are that you will be understood. A friend of mine speaks English in this Japanized manner and many think he is a fluent speaker of Japanese.

As other Japanese words, borrowed words are often abbreviated to facilitate communication. Listening to the radio, I was puzzled when the disc jockey announced that a familiar tune was the *santora* version. What? I had never heard of a label or group called *santora*. It soon became clear that the song was from a movie soundtrack, *saundo* from "sound" combining with *torraku* from "track" to render *santora*.

Japanese go further and recombine the English to create words that are new and attention getting. Since "Miss" (*missu*) signifies a female, so "MissWash" is logical for a product to clean a certain female undergarment. Walkman is a masterpiece of this branding with recombined English— so successful, in fact, it quickly became nearly a generic product name in the West.

But not all English words are suitable for adaptation; they must sound right. Japanese are very sensitive to onomatopoeia, for example, which seem to be capable of generating multiple images, an atmosphere. A person nodding off in the warm sun is in the state of *uto-uto*, but the image here is more than just that of physical slumber; it is rather one of psychological somnolence—oblivious and drifting.

To really understand this "feeling" of sound, perhaps we should listen to the Japanese. Composer Jun Sakurai explains that the name Marilyn Monroe is a lot sexier in Japanese than Brigitte Bardot. The *m* sound is made by parting of lips, which creates an inviting image—you don't have to understand Freud to get that! But the *b* sound is associated with the oral ejection and therefore has much less sexual appeal.

So here are extra dimensions to consider while exploring these English-sounding brand names and advertising phrases. Is a name sexy because it starts with *ma* or perhaps refreshing because it starts with a *sa*? Examined in this light, we can see

MEIDI-YA'S
フランクフルト
ソーセージ
Frank Furter Sausage
JAS
盛り合わせ
My As soon as you open this can, your delicious meal is ready. Have a great time.

that the connotations and emotional impact of Japanized words have little to do with their original English meanings, and our Western penchant for literal correctness is of little help in understanding them. But communicating without recourse to the literal is a consummate Japanese art, one which *Japanese Jive* now gives readers ample opportunity to experience, while, incidentally, having a great deal of fun.

George Fields is a long-time chronicler of Japanese consumer habits and author of *From Bonsai to Levis: When West Meets East* and *Gucci on the Ginza: Japan's New Consumer Generation*. Founder and CEO of ASI Market Research Japan, he is currently visiting professor at the Wharton School of the University of Pennsylvania.

"A distant chain saw cut into the birdsong; the rising wind whipped blue butterflies with stalks of goldenrod."

QUIZ

Brown Gross Foam is:

A hair-coloring mousse.

B used in the home to clean any-thing brown and gross.

C a novelty item—squirt a pile on the carpet at a cocktail party and watch the host go berserk (also works well at pool parties).

D is a non-nutritive, chocolate substitute.

Answer: A . Do you think it should read "Gloss" and not "Gross"? Those "l's" and "r's" are tricky!

Dew Dew

Why else does "an apple a day keep the doctor away"?

Fried Candy

Candy isn't exactly what comes to mind upon inspecting the contents of this bag *(below)*.

Dios Beer-Flavored White Chocolate

Hankerin' for a cold one, but you're the designated driver tonight? Don't despair. Enjoy your brew as it was meant to be served: solidly sandwiched between layers of creamy, white chocolate. Nothing tastes as smooth.

Suntory Beer Cocktail Fruit in Beer *(banana flavor)*

Banana beer? Hey, don't knock it 'til you try it. OK, you can knock it once you've stopped vomiting. (Orange and grapefruit flavors also available.)

"With Beer" Select Menu for Beer Time

"A stimulating companion for those special times that begin with beer. A select menu for adults with discerning tastes."

Serve this with soda pop and *suffer the consequences.*

IT IS A CHOCO MUSHI BREAD, WHICH IS MILD
AND MELLOW TO THE TASTE.

Chocolate Collon

Sounds repulsive, but *look* at it. If you were to graphically represent a colon in the form of candy, wouldn't it end up looking a lot like this?

Choco Mushi Bread

"It's a choco mushi bread which is mild and mellow to the taste."

Nothing can be quite as intimidating as chocolate-flavored bread. The Japanese people know this and have, therefore, developed their own kinder, gentler version of the potentially frightening treat. Theirs is "mushi," not firm; "mild and mellow," not rich or robust. Finally, eating chocolate bread is safe again.

Chocolate-Covered Mini Tree Stump Cookies

What child doesn't like tree stumps? In Japan adults love them, too! This candy brings back happy memories of their days in the mandatory teen log-felling squads.

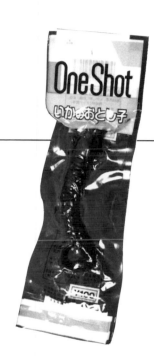

Fish ham is made by special Japanese techniques and has been enjoyed in Japan for more than 35 years. It has become very popular recently due to a renewed interest in low fat, low calorie health foods.

TS TOYO SUISAN

One Shot

Mid-afternoon stomach rumblings can be quickly quelled by just One Shot—of squid! Perfect for those times when eight legs and a torso are simply too much. Marinated, then neatly shrink-wrapped for portable, emergency snacking.

Almond Fish

Still not satisfied? Pop a few packets of **Almond Fish**. Tiny, dehydrated fish add a festive dose of protein to snack-time, especially if you're nuts about seafood.

Fish Ham

Your worst culinary nightmare . . .

Rare Cheese Pie

A pie is so rare that each comes with a registration number, certificate of purchase and commemorative photo suitable for framing.

Hi-Soft
(yogurt sour milk flavor)

Is it a trick or a treat?

Cheddar Cheese Candy

"This candy has made a reproduction of the nice flavor and rich taste of cheddar cheese."

The candy that made Wisconsin famous.

Flake Shake

Tired of ordinary fast food shakes? Stop by Mos Burger [*sic*] and pick up the **Flake Shake**: vanilla soft ice cream topped with rice cereal flakes and sweet red beans. A welcome relief from the delicious.

Crunky Kids is:

A a mild sedative for kids when they get rambunctious.
B the one and only candy shaped like children.
C crunchy chocolate nuggets.
D a clothing line for chubby children.

Answer: C

Vermont Curry

If it's curry from Vermont, you know it's authentic.

Crême Brulée Chocolate Bar

This candy bar won last year's Most Ludicrous Food award in the international "Let's Offend the French" competition.

Mille-Feuilles Chocolate Bar

Scrumptious pastries can't fit in your purse, but this condensed candy bar version sure can. Who cares about taste when convenience is all that matters?

Tiramisu Cream Cheese Chocolate

The flavor of Italian pudding is easy to enjoy when it's captured in a convenient candy bar.

QUIZ

Miss Tissue:

A blots lipstick for a marvelous matte finish.
B is used before dates.
C absorbs annoying facial oil build-up.
D is gentle for blowing delicate female noses.

Answer: B. And you darned well know where, too.

Miss Walk is:

A a close personal friend of Miss Tissue and Misswash.
B massaging pantyhose.
C foot deodorant.
D an attractive walking stick for women, with built-in mace.

Answer: C

Misswash:

A cleans dishes to the shine.
B is an intimate, feminine personal hygiene product.
C is a revolutionary, new, deep-cleanser for pores.
D cleans women's underwear at certain times of the month.

Answer: D. Woe to the brazen male who tries to use Misswash on a non-female stain.

White Water

And what other color of water might be suitable for consumption?

Plain White Water

Just like regular **White Water** but without all the frills.

Strawberry Water

Slightly less white than ordinary **White Water**.

Yodel Water

Volume Up Water

Swiss Concert in a Glass was developed by homesick Swiss expatriates living in Japan. Recipe for *Concert in a Glass:*

>One part **Volume Up Water**
>Two parts **Yodel Water**

Shake. Pour into a tall tumbler. Adjust volume to taste. Yodel like a maniac.

NFL Styling Grease

For the four-hours-inside-a-synthetic-helmet-sweaty-head look without all the effort!

Wet Mousse Super Dry Recipe

"A new concept in self-care, a complete plan to shape up a man's looks, set up a man's hair, tone up a man's appeal."

"Conceived and created for men."

Official mousse of the Confused Men's Movement.

"Hair Blow to Your Heart's Content"

The first hair care product made just for obsessive-compulsive stylists.

Babe Soda Candy

Preferred by gigolos worldwide, babe.

Buku Buku Candy

WARNING: This candy fizzes powerfully enough to knock over fat people.

Fibe-Mini

"A full day's supply of dietary fiber. Enjoy your day."

Of course you'll enjoy your day if you're clueless enough to think that 100 ml of sugary, orange water is going to give you a full day's dose of dietary fiber. If getting fiber were so tasty and easy, why would there be shredded wheat?

Hope Cigarettes

Peace Cigarettes

For those who wish to remain optimistic and calm in the face of lung cancer.

Little Bob Dog Candy Cigarettes

Shame on you, Little Bob Dog!

Salsa de Crispy

After about five minutes, it's going to taste more like Salsa de Soggy.

Blue Jeans Sausage

Happiness is a pocketful of portable pork.

Dried Bacon

His 'n' Hers

Garlic Potato Chips for Men

Hawaiian Barbecue Potato Chips for Women

It might seem that gender stratification has reached new levels of lunacy with these snacks, but wait—it's a proven fact that only women's pheromones react favorably to tropical barbecue flavors and only men's to garlic.

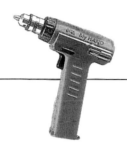

My Coffee **My Hand** **My Juice** **My Heart Bread**

It's certainly easier to sell more if everyone must have their own. Is this marketing genius or are the Japanese just naturally possessive?

"Not only quench our thirst through perspiration,

but supplement vitamin C positively."

おいしく健康、自然派スナックチョコ

LOTTE
CEREAL
CHOCOLATE

Creamy Powder
Creap
クリープ

クリープは
乳製品で
できています

ホワイトウォーター キャンデー
white water
Water feeling powder is in the center of the
white candy. Round blue chips are around it. Pretty, cute candy.

さわやか乳酸菌
キャンデーで

Blood Type Condoms

In Japan, blood type is supposed to determine your personality: A, sensitive; B, temperamental; AB, complex; O, extroverted. But which partner's blood type determines the condom you buy? A mistake could be fertile.

Super Winky:

This product:
A   renews energy to tired eyelids.
B   is the baby doll that winks.
C   is a funky brake-light attachment for your car.
D   is a brand of condom.

Answer: D

美しい網目、形状、芳香、豊潤な甘
味のマスクメロンは、グルメと作り手の
切磋琢磨が生んだ芸術品と言えるで
しょう。

★特選マスクメロン詰合せ
① **16,000**円 M-810-1052 ② **20,000**円 M-810-1063

Melon Milk

"Mom, are you kidding?

*"**Melon Milk** doesn't sound great, my dear."*

"Just try, then you will love it."

Hey, kid! Listen to your mother.

Gift Melons

Spending less than $180.00 on gift-boxed melons is just plain tacky (￥110＝$1.00).

Mama Pockety

Mama leaves your dishes smelling as fresh as carrots!

Clean Life, Please

Clean Kitchen Delicious Time Bags *(tea filters)*

"Clean Kitchen makes every day delicious."

Not just happy proverbs but maxims for the world's most anal-retentive culture.

Beverages or Bodily Fluids?

Calpis Water

My Morning Water

Yogurina Water

Vitamin Party

Ten fruits and ten vitamins—sounds like a party!

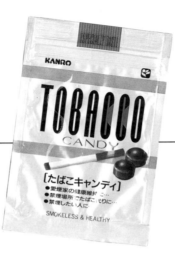

Tobacco Candy

Give the kids an early start on a nasty habit.

Dokudami

This beverage:

A   facilitates festive euthanasia.
B   promotes good health.
C   can only be served at wakes.
D   is a highly effective weight-loss
    shake.

Answer: B. The party-skeleton makes no bones about the intent of this beverage.

QUIZ

Milk Ball is:

A   a cream-filled bun.
B   a cow that needs to be milked immediately.
C   the Japanese Dairy Association's annual gala.
D   the baseball term for a wimpy pitch.

Answer: A

Milky

Leaves your hair looking, feeling, and smelling as fresh as milk.

Yogurt Fizz

Kudos to the bartender who finally discovered that yogurt, alcohol, and carbonation makes *the perfect* cocktail.

Glico gum Kiss Mint
グリコ **キスミントガム**

チェリーミント

● 眠気スッキリ、
新・ドライバー用ガム

The fragrant mint, natural caffeine, and delightful cherry aroma wake you up and keep you alert yet relaxed. The

perfect treat for drivers, students and workers who must work hour after hour.

FOR DRIVER

CHERRY MINT

Glico gum Kiss Mint
グリコ **キスミントガム**

● さわやか森林浴、
リラックス用ガム

The natural taste is like a fresh forest breeze. Perfect for a

break after work or study. With chlorophyll and natural flavorings.

FOR RELAX

森林の香り

100 円
(税別)

Glico gum Kiss Mint
グリコ **キスミントガム**

ライチ&レモン

● 気分さわやか、
リフレッシュ用ガム

A delicate blend of lemon and litchi flavors is enhanced by chondroitin for a dazzling

taste. It's good for refreshing mind and body.

FOR REFRESH

LITCHI & LEMON

100 円
(税別)

KISS

● お口が香る、
エチケット用ガム

Be up on your etiquette! The crisp clean apple fragrance keeps your breath always fresh

FOR

100 円
(税別)

Kiss Me!

Mint

グリコ **キスミントガム**

アップルミント

and clean. Perfect for dates and important interviews.

Glico **gum**

Kiss Mint

●香りエレガンス、 お口の香り用ガム

The fragrance that moves around you. With the refreshing harmony of jasmine and

グリコ **キスミントガム**

ジャスミン ミント

vitamin. Take with you for dates and get-together.

FOR ELEGANCE

JASMINE MINT

Kiss Mint

The **Kiss Mint** series has a gum for any situation you might possibly encounter, at least in Japan. Each variety offers an embellished description of its ingredients and a helpful essay suggesting the most appropriate circumstance for its consumption. For some reason elegant gum-chewing has yet to catch on in the USA.

Coffee Jelly

If you're *really* in a hurry, you can have your coffee *on* your toast.

Strawberry Cereal Chocolate

A tooth-rotting part of your balanced breakfast.

Hello Kitty Pre-Buttered Toast

Kitty's been thoughtful enough to pre-butter this slice of toast for lazy little children.

Mouth Jazz is:

A   adult-strength mouthwash.
B   the first musical chewing gum.
C   lip balm for trumpet players.
D   a lozenge once popular with
     beatniks.

Answer: A

**Partner with Your Mouth
Before . . .**

Breath-freshener for the grammatically impaired.

Mouth Pet is a:

A   soft, gentle toothbrush.
B   stimulating dental floss.
C   toothpaste that contains small
     plaque-fighting bacteria that,
     when magnified, resemble
     dachshunds.
D   breath freshener.

Answer: D

QUIZ

Family Whip is:

A   an S&M game for the whole family.

B   a computer tutorial guaranteed to increase user's IQ by 15 points.

C   non-dairy dessert topping.

D   a penal method unique to Japan whereby a neighborhood is allowed to inflict corporal punishment upon a particularly naughty family.

Answer: C

Shunmale

Preferred by radical feminists and women "in comfortable shoes."

QUIZ

Creap:

A   whitens coffee.

B   is a form-fitting pair of underpants that *doesn't* creep up.

C   is *the* magazine for private investigators.

D   kills creeping bathroom mildew.

Answer: A. There must be a more appealing acronym for "creamy powder."

Choco-Flake Light

Been eating too many chocolate-covered corn flakes lately? Thank goodness for **Choco-Flake Light**. It's got that scrumptious mix of corn and waxy, imitation chocolate, but with half the calories.

High Grade Dainty Roasted Crabs

What could be more dainty than a brimming mouthful of crunchy crab shells?

Soup-Sand Series

Eating soup with your fingers was always difficult—until Mini-Stop's new **Soup-Sand Series** came along. A generous serving of soup (gumbo or corn chowder) is encased in a golden, deep-fried, crumb crust and then placed on a pasty, white bun with mayonnaise and lettuce so it resembles any other fast-food sandwich. But one bite will tell you, as the Soup-Sand dribbles down your chin, that *this is no ordinary sandwich!*

QUIZ

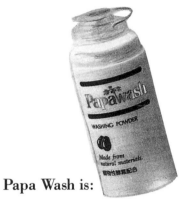

Papa Wash is:

A   shampoo for expectant fathers.
B   papaya-pulp facial cleanser.
C   masculine-scent soap.
D   the male parent of Misswash.

Answer: B. Someone left out the rather important "-ya."

My Wet

. . . because wetness is *such* a personal matter.

QUIZ

Wets is:

A   a baby-doll that teaches children about bladder control.
B   the Japanese brand name for adult diapers.
C   a refreshing beverage.
D   a fungal infection brought on by the rainy season in Japan.

Answer: C

Need Up Gel is:

A   a temporary cure for im-
     potence.
B   caffeinated lip salve.
C   an anti-depressant.
D   a hair product for anti-gravity
     styles.

Answer: D

Nice Stick

Nice Stick

The friendliest baguette in all the land.

Virgin Pink Special

Virgin Pink Special:
A   gives you baby-pink skin.
B   is a non-alcoholic drink.
C   restores virginity.
D   is virgin wool from a flock of
     mutant sheep.

Answer: A

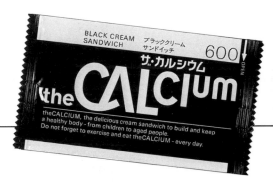

Super Black

How much blacker can you get?

**The Calcium
Black Creme Sandwich**

"The Calcium, the delicious cream sandwich to build and keep a healthy body—from children to aged people. Do not forget to exercise and eat The Calcium—every day."

How could anyone forget to eat some delicious black cream every day?

Black Black

Petit Meal *(prune flavor)*

Studies have shown that by far the most nutritionally complete instant breakfast drink is prune chunks floating in milk.

No Time

If you really have no time to brush, maybe you need to rearrange your priorities.

Marble Pocky Chocolate
(custard flavor)

"Marbled layers of milk chocolate and bittersweet chocolate grace this cookie-type Pocky made with eggs."

What on earth is a Pocky? And when did eggs become so exciting?

Save Water Tone

Ladies, embarrassing bodily noises in a deadly silent public restroom are history with the **Save Water Tone**, which produces a loud dose of white noise to replace wasteful "cover-up" flushing. Adjust the dial for the duration of noise you anticipate needing, press the start button and let loose! Save water *and* save face.

Washlet Multi-Function Toilet

"Because even people you like make smells."

Say goodbye to toilet paper with the Washlet. It squirts water from various angles to clean your most private parts and then blows you dry. The Washlet is also a sitz bath and a bidet. Aren't there some places from which high technology should just butt out?

Flush Handle—Weak/Strong

This clever toilet handle lets you choose the amount of flush water you need based on your performance.

Apple Crêpe

A plethora of preservatives gives this compact crêpe a shelf life of over 750 years. Cordon Bleu seal of approval still pending.

Every Burger

The inevitable outcome of the Japanese passion for American junk food and skill in miniaturization. Using space-age technology, a Japanese company has managed to shrink the cheeseburger to 1/93 its original size and radically alter its flavor to that of a sweet, sandwich-cookie, while maintaining the classic cheeseburger "look." Now, **Every Burger** in Japan tastes A-1.

Pretz (*salad flavor*)

Finally, a way to enjoy salad anytime, anywhere . . .

Trial-1

"Trial-1 is a drink which supplies water lost through perspiration. For sports, after a hot bath and hangover."

If you need to replace your ions after a hot bath, then perhaps it's time to switch to showers.

Relax Pipe
(grapefruit mint flavor)

Nothing calms the nerves like inhaling the tasty combination of grapefruit and mint through a plastic tube.

Diet Pipe

Forget diet shakes: hungry Japanese dieters know that sucking sweet potato flavor through a plastic tube is the surefire way to satisfy a craving. (Available in honey-lemon and coffee flavors, too.)

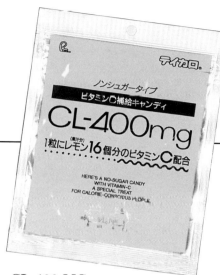

CL-400 MG

"Here's a no-sugar candy with vitamin C. A special treat for calorie-conscious people."

Every dieter's fantasy of a "special treat" is a pig-out party on vitamin C. And with a catchy name like CL-400 MG, you know it'll sell like hotcakes.

Hairmake

A baldness breakthrough! This shampoo actually grows new hair on barren heads . . . well, not really, but the name *is* misleading.

QUIZ

Sweatie is:

A a can of Pocari Sweat for kids.

B a descriptive name for dress shields.

C a sauna suit for water-weight loss.

D hair gel which gives men that macho "just finished working out" look.

Answer: B

Armpit Ray

Fashionable young Japanese women know that the key to popularity is a tan armpit.

Fever Beaver Pore Vacuum

Sucks out deep blackheads and impurities with the ferocity of a rabid rodent.

Humming Lady EX

Your breasts can be pert 'n' perky or sagging and pendulous with the breast-suction-fun-cone! **Humming Lady EX** creates any shape you desire. Have fun creating unique and exciting shapes all your own.

SURGEON GENERAL'S WARNING: Not for use during lactation.

Super-Cola

The caffeine in the cola makes you speak in explosive bursts.

Cutty Sark Candy

Originally developed for the astronauts' cocktail hour, now a treat available to all.

Honey and Lemon

"Take in reverse! Double Deposit candy."

WARNING: For best results, follow directions carefully.

Yogloo
(Fruit Basket Flavor)

The secret to Japanese longevity: a low-fat diet, lots of fiber and a bottle of yogurt-flavored gloo every morning.

Gambatte Kantaro
(Go for it, Mr. Liver!)

American hangover remedies have not been highly successful because they haven't used this new trick discovered by the Japanese: respectful anthropomorphism. That's right—address your liver with a modicum of courtesy like this bottle does, and your hangover woes are over.

Pudding Shake Creme Brulée

What could be more refreshing than a tall glass of chunky pudding?

Miss Peach Fizz

An exceptionally polite beverage gentle enough for young, single, inexperienced drinkers.

Smokey & Co. Whisky

The first whisky blended for gangs of junkyard dogs.

Air

For those seeking the ultimate in a light beverage.

Idaho Special

Hawaiian Delight

Tuna Special

イタリアン
ソーセージ、
フレッシュトマト、
ハラペニオ、チリソース、
オニオン、ペパロニ
FRESH TOMATO,
PEPPERONI, ONION, ITALIAN
SAUSAGE, CHILI SAUCE, JALAPENO
Ⓜ¥2,100 Ⓛ¥3,200
エスニックホット・ピザ
ETHNIC HOT PIZZA

Which is not an actual
Japanese pizza topping?

1. Short, naked [*sic*] clams
2. Potato salad
3. Marmalade
4. Boiled egg
5. Mayonnaise
6. Corned beef hash

Answer: 3 . Honest .

WHITE CREAM PIZZA
クリームソース・ピザ
Ⓜ¥1,900 Ⓛ¥2,800
オニオン、ピーマン、フレッシュ・マッシュ
ルーム、コーン、カナディアン・ベーコン
GREEN PEPPER, ONION, CORN,
CANADIAN BACON,
FRESH MUSHROOM

CURRY PIZZA
カレーソース・ピザ
Ⓜ¥1,900 Ⓛ¥2,800
オニオン、ピーマン、イタリアン・ソーセージ、
ポテトサラダ、タマゴ
ONION, GREEN PEPPER, BOILED EGG,
POTATO SALAD, ITALIAN SAU-
SAGE

Peculiar Pizza

Fit Fix Hot in Spa

"Creates a healthy bath with crude drugs that induce and accelerate perspiration. (Quasi-drug)"

One of a new line of narcotic toiletries, imported from Colombia.

Amand-Kiss Almond & Peanut Candy

"It includes much fragrant crushed almond and peanut inside just roasted, whose shape is like natural peanut. We think we can say this is only real nut candy."

We think we can say this candy talks too much.

Frank Furter Sausage

"As soon as you open this can, your delicious meal is ready. Have a great time."

Winner of the 1992 Most Courteous Processed Food award.

Greenwood

"Greenwood is for a gourmet who is sensitive to nature. Open this and you can feel and hear a forest breeze. The forest's fresh air gives Greenwood its gentle flavor."

Perhaps there's a little more than just marmalade in this jar.

Koeda Twig Chocolate

*"A lovely and tiny twig **Koeda** is a heroine's treasured chocolate born in the forest. The sentimental taste is cozy for the heroine's in the town."*

WARNING: Eating too much chocolate can play havoc with your syntax.

White Water Candy

"Water feeling powder is in the center of the white candy. Round blue chips are around it. Pretty, cute candy."

The candy for extremely confused, shallow people.

Fruit Festa

A special treat made from festering fruit!

Super Hard

One can only imagine . . .

Coffee on the Rock is:

A   a video game for Zen Buddhists.

B   a recent archaeological discovery in Gibraltar.

C   a copywriter's egregious omission.

D   Juan Valdez's theater of the absurd.

Answer: C

Le Roi Social Moisture Cream

Rub it in to cure nerdiness.

Nippless

For the woman (or man) with nothing more serious to worry about than the embarrassment of erect, visible nipples, here's the solution. Using masking tape to tame those pesky, pert nipples would just be too déclassé.

Whity

The beverage that's also a racial slur.

QUIZ

Arm Joy is:

A   a deodorant especially Ph-balanced for women.
B   a lightweight tennis racquet.
C   a depilatory for unsightly arm hair.
D   a vacuum cleaner.

Answer: D

Ha Wa Yu Card

The gift certificate that cares enough to ask, "Ha wa yu?"
"Why, I'm fine, thanks. And you?"

Live Asahi for Live People

Believe it or not, there *is* actually beer for dead people in Japan.

Calpis

Said aloud, **Calpis** sounds like the urine from either a) our friend the cow or b) major league baseball's cutest player, but in fact it's neither—it's a syrupy, sweet fermented milk drink. And with a name like **Calpis**, it's gotta be great fermented milk!

Jive Coffee

Shhh . . . don't tell. It's not really coffee—it's just jiving you.

Pocari Sweat

The most unfortunate name ever bestowed upon a beverage.

Café in Bottle

It's worth depleting the ozone layer for products as necessary as this one.

QUIZ

Secret Shoes:

A   are elevator shoes.
B   were worn by the emperor with his new clothes.
C   are ill-fitting shoes naughty children must wear as punishment.
D   is a game show in which contestants try to match celebrities with their shoes.

Answer: A

Orchard Story Cologne

"Nuts Taste"

Nothing drives men more wild with desire than the smell of nuts.

McPassport, the Japanese McDonald's Travel Service

Let McDonald's book your next trip to Europe and rest assured that you'll travel only with other junk-food junkies.

Gizua Waterproof Pantyhose

Women, eliminate the horror of wet legs with waterproof pantyhose. (Just imagine how comfortable it must be to wear these for ten hours straight on a humid summer day.)

Amnesty International Pajamas

. . . in case you sleepwalk while in a totalitarian state.

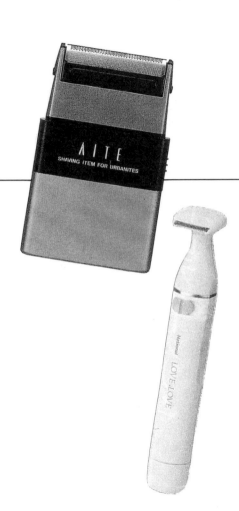

QUIZ

Aite for Urbanites

WARNING: Not to be used in the suburbs.

Love-Love

Encouragement from your razor helps you face the new day.

Armpit is:

A   an electric shaver for women's underarms.
B   a body part.
C   a trendy Tokyo boutique selling only tank tops.
D   a glue-on patch of underarm hair for men who appear less than hirsute.

Answer: A & B

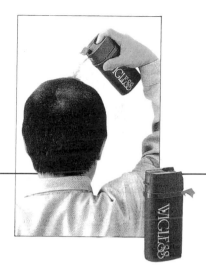

Cool Bathcrin

Gets your bathtub squeaky crin.

Fred MacMurray Store

Why is Fred MacMurray a cult figure among trendy Japanese teens?

Wigless

Wigless doesn't reveal its mysterious concealing chemical, but if you're cheap enough to use an aerosol spray to cover that fleshy pate, it's best not to ask too many questions.

Cow Brand Beauty Soap

. . . keeps you looking your bovine best.

Eye Talk

Tired of smooth Asian eyelids? One application of **Eye Talk** eyelid glue gives you creased eyelids that any Caucasian would envy. Glue lasts up to four hours. Nictitation was never so much fun.

Chocolate Bubble on Flavor

Good news for chocoholics: bathing in chocolate bubble bath is the no-calorie way to get your fix.

Cham-pe

Lemon Squash American

The Japanese Ministry of Trade and Industry (MITI) recently determined that there are not enough names for the hundreds of soft drinks now being produced in Japan and has, therefore, mandated the emergency use of the above nonsense names.

Posmic

WHIZZMAN

Oh!

東芝DynaBook/J-3100シリーズ
アプリケーション活用誌「オー！ダイ

平成5

平成5年7月1日発行 毎月1回1日発行・第16巻・第7号・通巻141号 昭和60年12月26日第三種郵便認可

FOOL'S MATE

YOUNG

週刊ヤングジャンプ

FINEBOYS

N

Remember Ne

Mad Magazines

Asa Can

Proper etiquette dictates that banana-flavored milk should only be served in the morning *(asa).*

Mild Time Stomach Friendly Coffee

"A new concept of coffee to match contemporary healthy life styles, which is gentle on your body."

Isn't it time you treated your stomach with more respect?

Calorie Mate

A product which violates the cardinal rule of the food industry—*calories have never been and will never be our friends.*

UCC Dutch Coffee

"We wish to give the customers much more relaxation. UCC creates the products with everlasting desire."

JO Coffee

"This coffee with the tasty aroma solely for the refined adult people."

Drip Coffee

"Drip coffee filtered through flannel."

There is a coffee to suit everyone's personality in Japan: whether you're refined, relaxed, or just a drip.

Regain

Maxim Instant Coffee

"The wood porch faced east. First sunrise burned the mist from the hilly hollows, then dried out the webs spiders spun overnight between leaves of grass. A distant chain saw cut into the birdsong; the rising wind whipped blue butterflies with stalks of goldenrod."

WARNING: Drinking too much coffee can cause paranoid delusions.

Did you think that Japan, Inc., came about because of some genetic predisposition the Japanese have for hard work? Nonsense! The secret is bottled stamina. **Regain** enables the salaryman* to work 24 hours straight, so its ingredients are guaranteed to be banned by the USFDA. The recent economic downturn has indicated that working 24 hours straight may not be enough. In response, the Regain company is now marketing **Regain 48.**

Real Gold

Another stay-up-all-night product, but this one has the added goodness of liquid nicotine. As if salarymen didn't get enough from chain-smoking.

"Salaryman" is the Japanese term for a male, white collar employee.

Dolce Vita Hotel-Made Ice Cream

You can't mistake that mass-produced taste . . .

Koala Ice Cream

Koalas and chocolate ice cream—a tempting combination.

Royal Barrel Ice Cream

Scraped right out of her majesty's private stock.

Single Plug-In Curler

You knew that Japanese apartments are small, but did you know that some are so small that they allow women room enough for only a single, electric hair curler?

Slim Spray

And you thought it was because they ate a lot of rice and fish.

Arvina Cool Milk Lotion

"Application of aerobics to skin cells creates lush and healthy skin."

The fitness craze has hit Japan so hard that there are now aerobics classes for even the lowly skin cell.

Enough Said

The Strawberry Milk

The Coffee

The Curry

HOP STEP!

NOBODY KNOWS WHERE IT IS.
THAT'S A HUGE AND SILENT PLACE.

Underpants

*"Nobody knows where it is.
That's a huge and silent place."*

Perhaps a lesson in basic anatomy might help the baffled author of this suggestive copy.

Disclaimer

Product names and ad copy featured in *Japanese Jive* were taken verbatim from the packaging of actual products available to Japanese consumers; absurd commentary and silly quizzes are entirely products of the author's imagination. It is our hope that readers will enjoy sorting out the real from the fictitious.